BEGINNING SIGN LANGUAGE SERIES

SIGNING AT SUNDAY SCHOOL

Designed and illustrated by
Jane Schneider, Marina Krasnik, and Kathy Kifer

Special thanks to

BJ Hauck
for her help and guidance

Copyright © 1998 by Stanley H. Collins

Published by
Garlic Press
605 Powers Street
Eugene, OR 97402

www.garlicpress.com

ISBN 0-931993-99-7
Reorder Number GP-099

Introduction

Signing at Sunday School should be used as a helpful signing guide in the Sunday School setting. It provides both hearing impaired and hearing children a common ground for their exchanges and their worship. Songs, the story of Jesus, and Bible verses are fully illustrated and easy to follow.

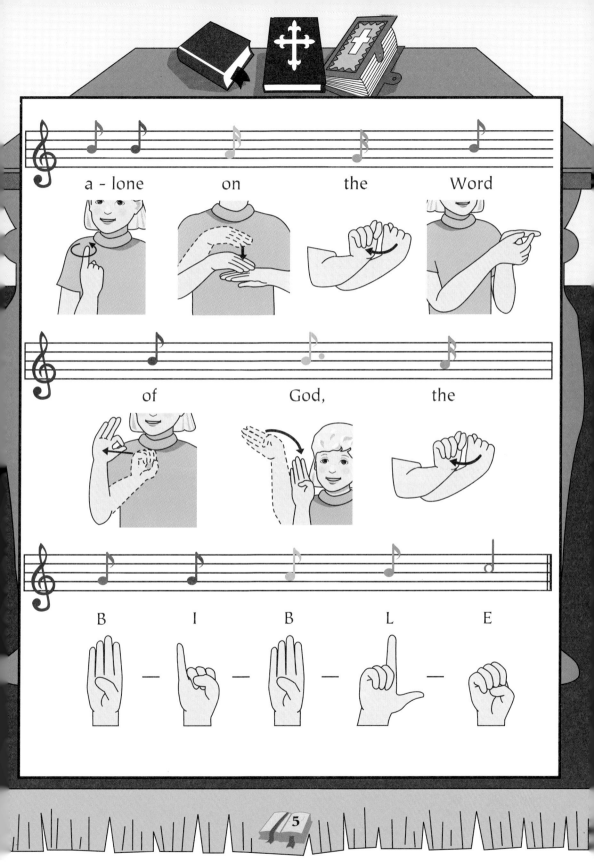

a - lone   on   the   Word

of   God,   the

B — I — B — L — E

Jesus Loves Me

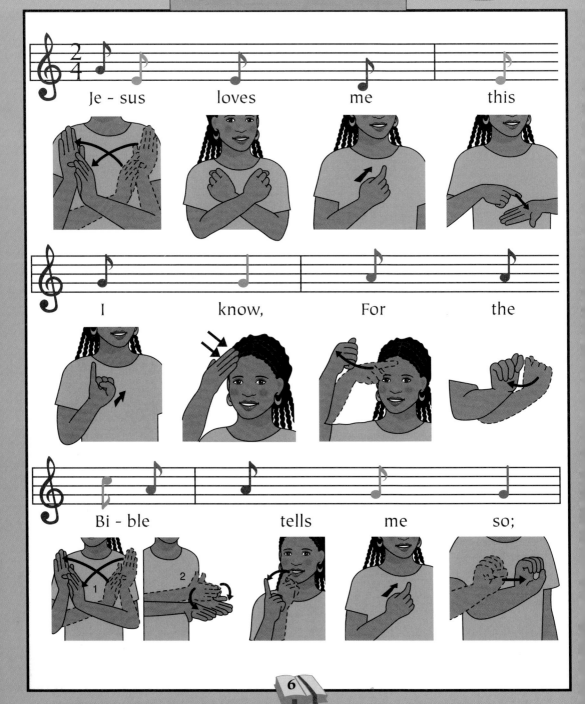

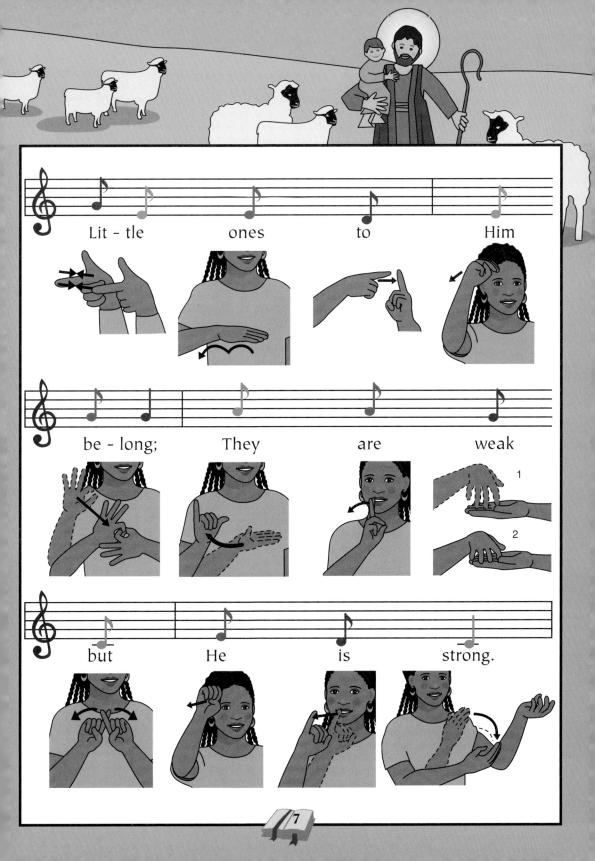

Lit - tle   ones   to   Him

be - long;   They   are   weak

but   He   is   strong.

7

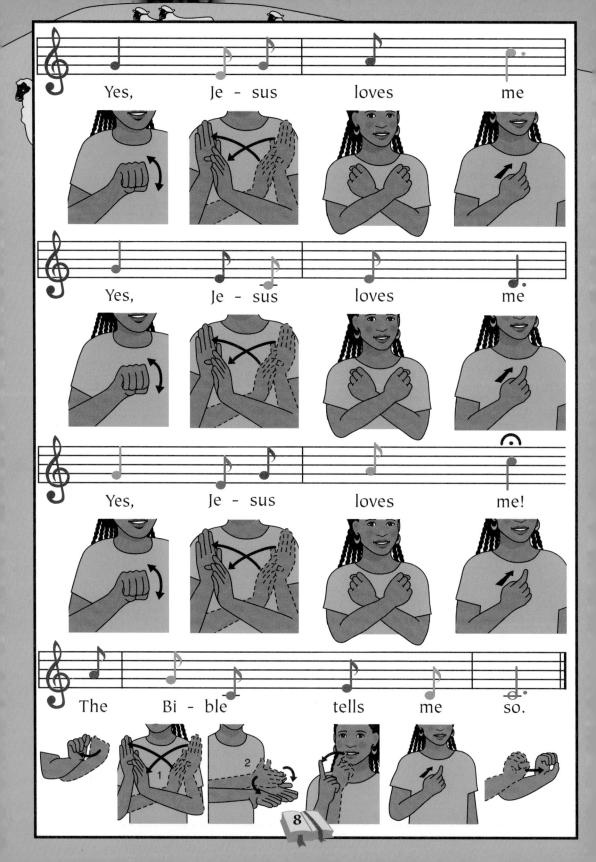

Jesus Loves the Little Children

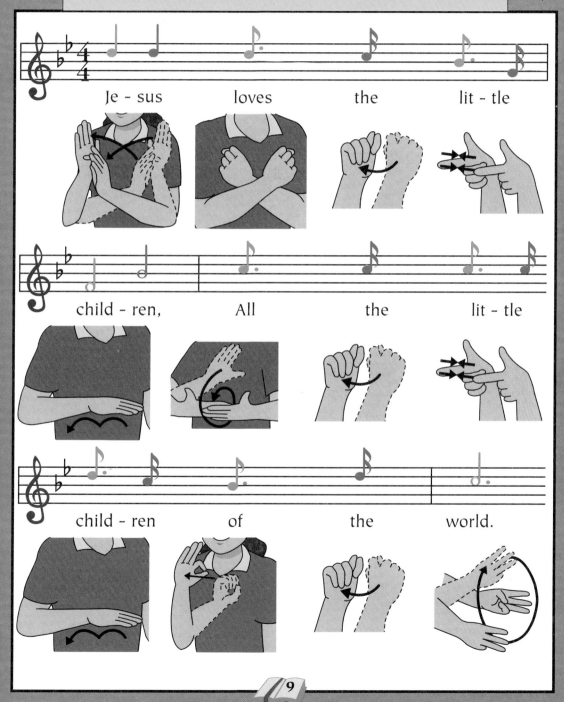

Je - sus   loves   the   lit - tle

child - ren,   All   the   lit - tle

child - ren   of   the   world.

Red ... and ... yel - low, ... black

and ... white, ... They ... are

pre - cious ... in ... His ... sight;

10

Je - sus   loves   the   lit - tle

chil - dren   of   the   world.

Angel tell

Mary she have

God's son. His

name Jesus.

An angel told Mary she was having
God's son. His name would be Jesus.

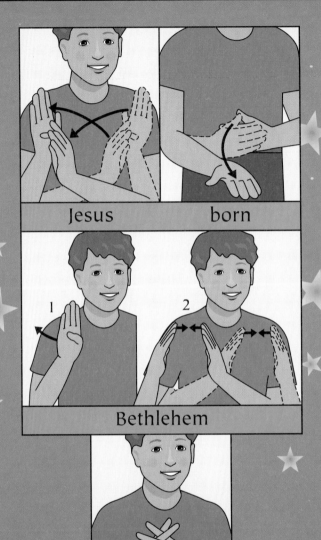

Jesus

born

Bethlehem

manger

Jesus was born in Bethlehem in a manger.

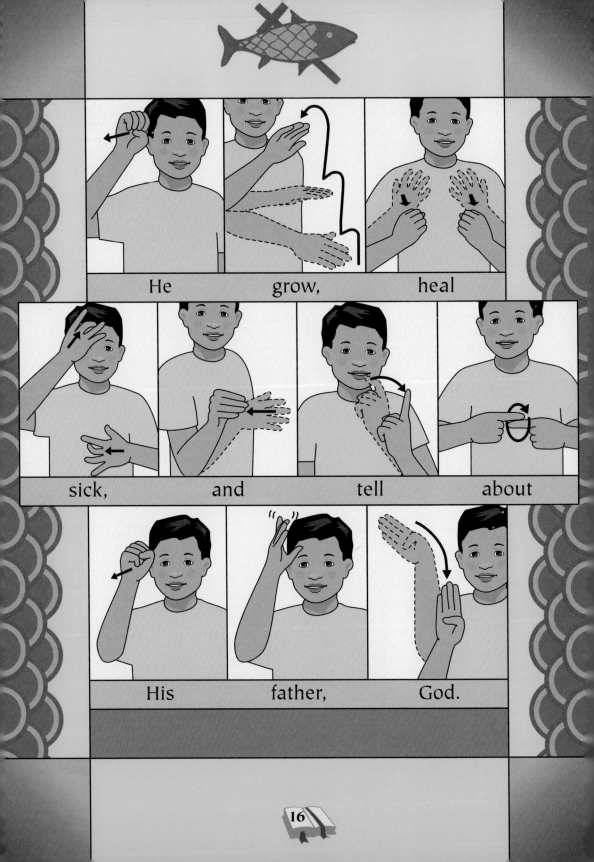

He grow, heal

sick, and tell about

His father, God.

He grew up, healed the sick,
and told about His father, God.

 17

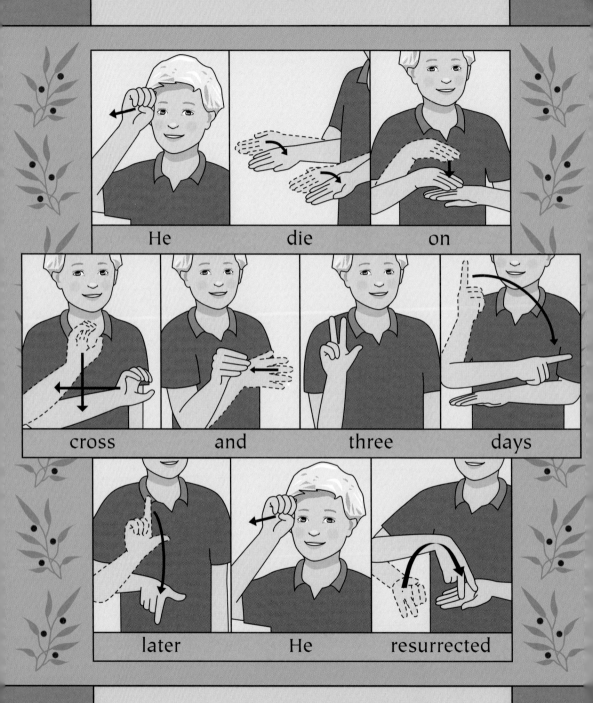

He   die   on

cross   and   three   days

later   He   resurrected

He died on a cross and
three days later He was resurrected.

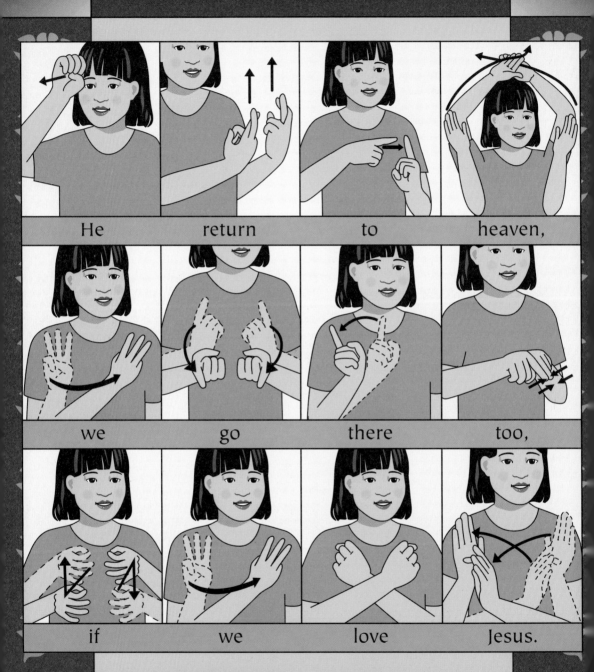

He	return	to	heaven,
we	go	there	too,
if	we	love	Jesus.

He went back to heaven
and we'll go there too, if we love Jesus.

Matthew 5:3-10

be   pure,   bring

peace,   and   God   will

be   with   you.

Luke 6:31
The Golden Rule

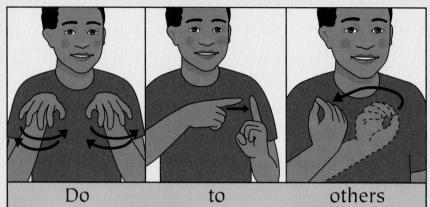

Do to others

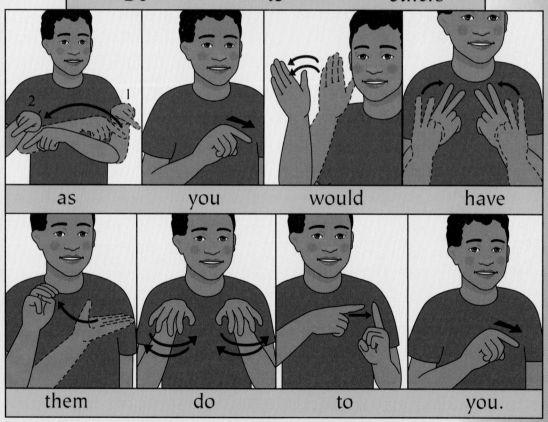

as you would have

them do to you.

Proverbs 3:5

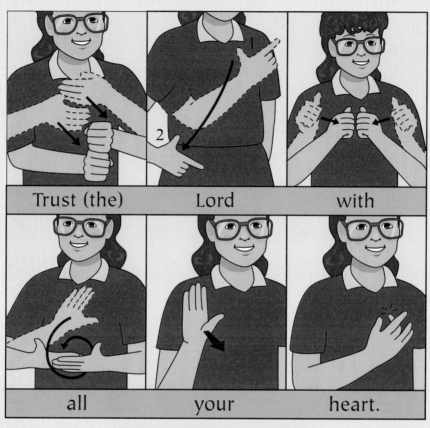

Trust (the)	Lord	with
all	your	heart.

Corinthians 13: 4, 6-8

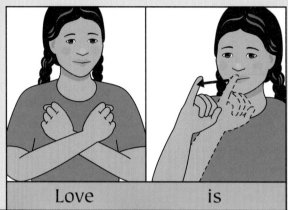

Love   is

patient.   Love   is

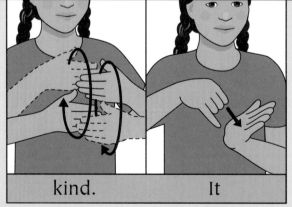

kind.   It

is   full

of   joy   when (the)

truth   is

Corinthians 13: 4, 6-8 (continued)

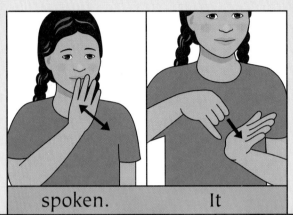

spoken.   It

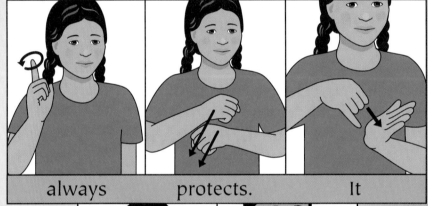

always   protects.   It

always   trusts.

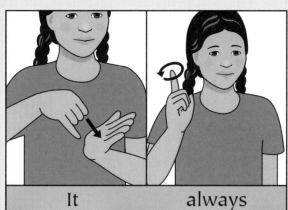

It   always

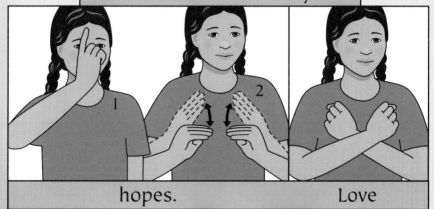

hopes.   Love

never   fails.

Index

Also from Garlic Press

Finger Alphabet GP-046
Uses word games and activities to teach the finger alphabet.

Signing in School GP-047
Presents signs needed in a school setting.

Can I Help? Helping the Hearing Impaired in Emergency Situations
GP-057 Signs, sentences and information to help communicate with the hearing impaired.

Caring for Young Children: Signing for Day Care Providers and Sitters
GP-058 Signs for feelings, directions, activities and foods, bedtime, discipline and comfort-giving.

An Alphabet of Animal Signs
GP-065 Animal illustrations and associated signs for each letter of the alphabet.

Mother Goose in Sign
GP-066 Fully illustrated nursery rhymes.

Number and Letter Games
GP-072 Presents a variety of games involving the finger alphabet and sign numbers.

Expanded Songs in Sign
GP-005 Eleven songs in Signed English. The easy-to-follow illustrations enable you to sign along.

Foods GP-087
A colorful collection of photos with signs for 43 common foods.

Fruits & Vegetables GP-088
Thirty-nine beautiful photos with signs.

Pets, Animals & Creatures
GP-089 Seventy-seven photos with signs of pets, animals & creatures familiar to signers of all ages.

Signing at Church
GP-098 For adults and young adults. Helpful phrases, the Lord's Prayer and *John 3:16.*

Signing at Sunday School
GP-099 Phrases, songs, Bible verses and the story of Jesus clearly illustrated.

Coyote & Bobcat
GP-081 A Navajo story serving to tell how Coyote and Bobcat got their shapes.

Raven & Water Monster
GP-082 This Haida story tells how Raven gained his beautiful black color and how he brought water to the earth.

Fountain of Youth
GP-086 This Korean folk tale about neighbors shows the rewards of kindness and the folly of greed.

Ananse the Spider: Why Spiders Stay on the Ceiling
GP-085 A West African folk tale about the boastful spider Ananse and why he now hides in dark corners.

www.garlicpress.com